The Brahman and the Ungrateful Tiger

Retold by Alan Horsfield
Illustrations by Rob Mancini

PM Plus Chapter Books

Ruby

U.S. Edition © 2013 HMH Supplemental Publishers
10801 N. MoPac Expressway
Building #3
Austin, TX 78759
www.hmhsupplemental.com

Text © 2003 Cengage Learning Australia Pty Limited
Illustrations © 2003 Cengage Learning Australia Pty Limited
Originally published in Australia by Cengage Learning Australia

6 7 8 9 10 11   1957   14
18649

Text: Alan Horsfield
Illustrations: Rob Mancini
Printed in China by 1010 Printing International Ltd

The Brahman and the Ungrateful Tiger

ISBN 978 0 75 786888 7

Contents

A Broken Promise

Many years ago, in India, tigers roamed the countryside. They were feared by villagers and by farmers, because they attacked animals and were a constant danger to people. Whenever they could, the people would capture tigers and put them in cages.

One day, a Brahman priest was walking barefoot along a hot, dusty road, when he came across a big tiger who was trapped in a bamboo cage.

The tiger knew that Brahmans were kind, gentle people. He called to the holy man, "Brother Brahman, do not look away. Have pity on me and release me from this miserable cage."

The Brahman saw that the tiger was sweltering in his cramped cage.

The tiger pleaded with the Brahman. "It is hot in the sun, and I have been locked up since sunrise," he said. "I am very thirsty. Please let me out."

The Brahman walked around the cage and looked pityingly at the unhappy tiger. He shook his head and said, "I cannot let you out of the cage. If I did, you would certainly eat me."

The Brahman was about to continue on his way when the tiger protested. "That cannot be true," he said. "How could a man such as you think so badly of me? Do you think that I would be so ungrateful?"

The kind-hearted Brahman hesitated. It was his duty to help all creatures. But he could not help feeling afraid of the tiger.

"Let me out for just a moment, please," begged the tiger. "The day is hot. Once I have had a drink from the river, I will return immediately to my cage."

The worried Brahman considered the tiger in his hot, cramped cage. He took pity on the poor beast. "I see that you are suffering," he said. "I will let you out of the cage – but first you must promise not to harm me."

The tiger hid a smile and said, "I will not harm you. I promise."

The Brahman, trusting the tiger's words, untied the twine knot that held the cage door securely shut. Then he pulled the door open.

No sooner was the door opened than the tiger eased himself from the cage. He stood slowly and stretched his aching limbs. Then he turned to the Brahman. "I am hungry as well as thirsty," he growled meanly. "I will *eat* before I drink."

The tiger stalked menacingly toward the Brahman. He crouched, ready to spring ...

A Dangerous Agreement

The frightened Brahman held up his hands in alarm and stepped back. "My friend, you promised not to harm me," he stammered. "I trusted your word, but you have tricked me. I set you free from your horrible little cage, and now you threaten to eat me."

"Did I trick you?" sneered the tiger. "Have I broken my promise? Am I ungrateful? My dear friend, I have never met a human who kept a promise. I have never met a human who was grateful. Why should I, a simple tiger, keep my promise to a human? Why should I be grateful to a human? Humans are the most ungrateful creatures on this earth!"

"Wait!" cried the Brahman. "Don't be so hasty. It is not fair to say that *all* humans are ungrateful. It is true that *some* humans are ungrateful, but there are many who are not. Many keep their promises. It would be unfair to punish me because some humans make mistakes.

"But I can see that you will not take my word for it. We should ask the opinion of five witnesses."

"What would that prove?" growled the impatient tiger.

"If any of the witnesses agree that you should keep your promise to me because humans are *not* ungrateful, then you shall let me continue my journey," explained the Brahman.

The tiger looked doubtful. "Why should I agree to that?" he growled.

The Brahman continued. "But if all five witnesses agree that humans *are* ungrateful, then it is only fair that you should have your way," he said humbly.

"Oh, very well," agreed the tiger. "Let's ask five witnesses if they believe that humans can be trusted to keep their word. Or if humans are ever grateful to those who have helped them."

The tiger looked around impatiently. "Look," he growled, "there's an old ox sleeping in a field, under a banyan tree. He can be the first witness."

The First Witness

The Brahman and the tiger went over to the ox.

"My friend," said the Brahman, "please help us. When I first saw the tiger, he was in a bamboo cage. He was suffering from thirst. He pleaded with me to release him, and promised to do me no harm. But when I opened the cage, he threatened to eat me! What, friend ox, do you think? Should the tiger keep his word? Is it right that he should be so ungrateful?"

The ox slowly opened his big eyes. "Ungrateful? You, a human, complain that the tiger is ungrateful?" he grumbled. "Humans are the most ungrateful creatures on this earth!"

The tiger smiled.

"Look at me," the ox continued. "When I was young, I served my master well. I pulled a plow through the hard soil. I pulled a heavy cart to the village market. My master praised me for my strength, and promised me fine rewards. But now I am old, and he has forgotten all of my hard labors for him. He brought me here to this field, and left me alone, because he no longer had any use for me! I fear that I will die of loneliness."

The ox turned to the tiger and said, "Eat him, brother tiger. He does not deserve your gratitude. Humans, of all creatures, are the most ungrateful."

Then the old ox closed his eyes and continued his sleep.

The tiger smiled with delight. This was what he had wanted to hear. "Well, my dear Brahman," he said to the holy man, "our friend the ox agrees that humans *are* ungrateful. He agrees that I should not keep my promise to you. So I will eat you now, before I grow any hungrier."

The Banyan Tree

The tiger lunged toward the Brahman. "Wait!" cried the holy man. "You are in too much of a hurry. The ox was only the first witness. We have four more to go."

The tiger looked dissatisfied. "I cannot wait forever!" he growled impatiently. "We will ask this banyan tree."

The Brahman turned to the gnarled old banyan tree that the ox was sleeping under, and called, "Banyan tree, did you hear my story? Should the tiger keep his word? Is it right that he should be so ungrateful?"

The old tree replied wearily, "I have big thick leaves that give shade to villagers and peasants. The shade protects them from the fierce sun of summer. But do they ever thank me? No! They take my shade for granted. Often when they rest in my shade, they break my branches and take my leaves. I do not like humans. They are very ungrateful!"

At these words the tiger laughed out loud. "You see, my friend," he said, "no living thing likes your kind. Prepare to meet your fate." He sharpened his claws and prepared to strike the Brahman.

The shocked Brahman stepped back. "No, no!" he cried. "We agreed that it should be five witnesses. We have to find three more."

"Two or five," snorted the tiger, "it will all be the same! However, we shall continue."

They left the ox and the banyan tree, and walked along the hot road, until they met a donkey.

The Brahman asked the donkey to listen to his tale, and the puzzled donkey agreed.

For the third time, the Brahman told his story – how he had trusted the tiger's word, and how he had been tricked.

All the while, the tiger prowled around in circles, impatient for the Brahman to finish.

Completing his story, the Brahman said, "I released the tiger from the cage so that he could get a drink. Is it fair that I should now become his meal?"

More Problems for the Brahman

The tired donkey looked at the tiger, and then at the Brahman. He brayed and twitched his ears as if he were thinking deeply.

"It *is* fair," he answered slowly. "When I was a young donkey, I carried many heavy loads of firewood, crops that had been harvested, and goods from the traders in town. In those days, my master fed me and took good care of me. I had hay to rest my bones on at night. I had shelter from the wind and rain.

"Now I am old and much slower, and he shouts at me. He threatens me with a stick, because I do not walk as fast as I used to. He gets angry and forgets to feed me or give me water. Is that fair? Is my master grateful for the many years of good service I gave him?"

The donkey snorted and shook his head at the Brahman. "Humans are the most ungrateful creatures on this earth!"

The tiger smirked.

The Brahman turned to the tiger and said, "It is true that there are many ungrateful humans. But not all humans are ungrateful. Let us find the last two witnesses."

The tiger looked impatiently at the Brahman, then strode off in front of him.

Shortly, they came to a river. A big crocodile was sunning itself on the muddy bank. The Brahman roused the crocodile and repeated his story.

The crocodile was not interested, but the Brahman insisted that he give an opinion.

"Very well," said the crocodile, "if you want my opinion, you shall have it! Many of my brothers, sisters, and cousins have been killed by humans who used their skins to make shoes and bags. We crocodiles are hunted for nothing more than our hides."

The crocodile looked up at the tiger and declared, "I say to you tiger, eat him before he and the rest of his kind can kill us all. We only want to live in peace!"

This made the tiger laugh loudly, but the Brahman just hung his head.

"Give up now," roared the tiger. "I have four witnesses out of five. No one likes your kind! The fifth witness will merely make it a certainty. It will be a waste of time."

The Jackal

At that moment, a jackal came along the road. The jackal and the tiger had never been friends. The tiger despised the scavenging ways of jackals.

However, as it was getting late and the tiger was anxious to have his meal, he ignored his past differences with the jackal.

"Let's finish this foolishness now," growled the tiger gruffly. He held up his paw and beckoned to the jackal.

The jackal stopped. "Jackal," the tiger bellowed, "kindly help us to settle a small disagreement."

The puzzled jackal agreed. Jackals rarely help tigers.

Again, the sad Brahman repeated his story. He told how he had trusted the tiger's word, and how he had been tricked. The jackal listened carefully.

When he had finished his tale, the Brahman said, "Friend jackal, do you think the tiger is being fair? Is it right that he should be so ungrateful?"

The Jackal
Seems Confused

The jackal looked thoughtfully at the Brahman, and scratched his paw in the dust for a moment or two. "What a strange story!" he said at last. "But I do not understand it. I am quite confused. Now, brother Brahman, as I see it, you were in the cage, and this good tiger set you free?"

The tiger looked at the jackal with disgust. "No," he growled, "*I* was in the cage!"

The jackal's eyes gleamed. "Ahh, now I understand! You and the Brahman were in the cage together and ... But that doesn't seem to make sense. Who let you out?"

The tiger sighed deeply.

The Brahman said, "No, no, friend jackal. This is what happened ..." And he told his sorry tale once more.

The jackal shook his head. "I still don't understand. Maybe it would be better if you showed me the cage?"

The tiger glared at the jackal. "You fool!" he cried. "You are wasting my time. But if you must see the cage, so be it!"

The tiger and the Brahman led the jackal to the cage. The jackal looked slyly at the Brahman. "Now, brother Brahman," he said, "where were you when you met the tiger?"

"I had just walked up this road, and I stood in front of the cage – just here," explained the Brahman.

The jackal scratched his chin and looked puzzled. "I see," he said. "But where was the tiger all this time?"

The tiger groaned. "I was *in the cage!*" he cried.

"*You* were in the cage?" said the jackal. "What on earth could *you* be doing in such a small cage? Were you standing up? Surely you were not lying down? I cannot believe that a tiger could fit into such a small cage!"

"It was very cramped!" snarled the tiger. "Let me show you." He squeezed back into the cage to show just how cramped he had been. He was becoming rather annoyed with the jackal.

"Oh," said the jackal with another sly look at the Brahman. "Now I'm starting to understand."

Back to Where We Started

The jackal stood silently for a moment, then turned again to the Brahman and said, "But the door is wide open! Why did the tiger need your help if the cage door was wide open like that?"

"It wasn't," explained the Brahman, who was also beginning to lose patience with the jackal's foolishness. "It was closed, and securely fastened with twine."

The jackal looked the Brahman in the eyes and said, "Then close and secure the door."

The Brahman suddenly understood what the jackal was up to. He closed the cage door with a bang, and tied it shut.

"Well, that's how it was!" said the jackal, nodding his head slowly. "We are now back to where we started, as I understand it."

The tiger suddenly felt afraid.

Then he was furious. The jackal had *tricked* him! He let out a loud, angry roar.

The jackal turned to the Brahman. "Brother Brahman," he said plainly, "I would advise you to think carefully before letting tigers out of cages, no matter how convincing their promises might sound. Humans can indeed be ungrateful, but there is nothing quite as dangerous as a hungry tiger."

The Brahman turned to look at the fuming tiger. "Well, my friend," he said, "I'll bet you're sorry you didn't keep your promise!"

When the Brahman turned back again, the jackal was already walking up the road, toward the setting sun. The Brahman had not had time to thank him.

The tiger groaned. He had again lost his freedom. Maybe this time forever.